To John Davis,
without whose tireless and unstinting rudeness
this book would not have been possible

Contents

Bad
Manners

The Complete Guide to Incredibly Rude Behavior for the 1990s

JOHN DAVIS

CB

CONTEMPORARY
BOOKS

CHICAGO

Library of Congress Cataloging-in-Publication Data

Davis, John, 1947–
    Bad manners : the complete guide to incredibly rude
behavior for the 1990s / John Davis.
        p.   cm.
    ISBN 0-8092-3938-8
    1. Human behavior—Humor.   2. Invective—
Humor.   3. Disorderly conduct—Humor.   I. Title.
PN6231.H763D38   1992
818'.5402—dc20   92-20188
                                                                    CIP

Published by Contemporary Books, Inc.
180 North Michigan Avenue, Chicago, Illinois 60601
Manufactured in the United States of America
International Standard Book Number: 0-8092-3938-8

Acknowledgments

I would be remiss if I did not gratefully acknowledge all the work of Tracy Mailloux in typing the manuscript for *Bad Manners*. Most especially, I thank my editor, Linda Gray, an absolute delight to work with and one who inspired me to new heights of brazen insolence.

Introduction

Fed up with straitlaced, endlessly exhaustive compendiums of deadening decorum, mind-numbing protocol, and unsatisfying, hopelessly outdated social conventions? Good. *Bad Manners* was written for you—and countless other long-suffering souls. Here's why.

You're faced with yet another indescribably awkward social situation. It's telethon time on your favorite TV station. Or it's the crack of dawn and another perky Jehovah's Witness has decided to ring your bell and save your soul. Maybe you're planning to spend the afternoon in court with your soon-to-be-ex-spouse. Understandably, you're at something of a loss as to the correct protocol. Where can you find the absolutely perfect language to vent your inflamed, tortured spleen? It's a delicate situation, etiquette-wise, and you need a pro. Fear not, because *Bad Manners* is here to save the day.

With this book, you too can learn to be crude, boorish, and memorable at virtually every social function, business meeting, or special occasion. Once you've mastered these time-tested recipes for insufferable rudeness, people all over town will cluck their tongues, roll their eyes, and gasp in amazement, overwhelmed by your bold yet clever incivilities.

You see, in some situations good manners just don't cut the cheese as far as personal satisfaction goes. Sometimes you need an alternative to the dictates of those tight-lipped society snobs who decide what you can and cannot do. *Bad Manners* is that alternative.

Airplane Flights

Tighten your seat belt and say your prayers. You'll have fellow passengers and flight personnel alike screaming "MAYDAY!" at the top of their lungs after employing these atrociously contemptible things to say and do during your next plane flight.

• Tell the flight attendant you want a window seat because you want to know immediately when "something falls off."

• During the review of safety procedures prior to takeoff, ask the flight attendant how much oxygen deprivation the artist suffered before he drew the illustration "that shows a two-thousand ton airplane floating on water long enough for the passengers and crew to evacuate safely."

• Ask the flight attendant why the life jackets are stamped "irregular," "reject," or "wholesale only."

• Mention loudly that you think it highly unlikely that, in the event of a crash landing any passengers

1

will have the superhuman strength to open a bent, thirty-five-hundred-pound exit door and then safely walk out onto the white-hot engine cowling to escape the billowing curtain of toxic fumes and superheated air.

• Advise the pilot that in the future you'd appreciate it if he would prepare his flight plan on something other than a cocktail-lounge napkin.

• Invite fellow passengers to sit on your lap, "so we can get the hang of it when the plane starts to crash."

• Help prepare for a crash-landing drill by

1. throwing food trays and personal luggage around the cabin;

2. blocking the exits with someone else's body; and

3. preparing a rough draft of your will.

• Ask loudly, "What's that ticking noise underneath that Palestinian guy's seat?"

• Tell the cabin attendant you need a "good cigar" and ask her if they have charts aboard to get you to Cuba.

• Inform fellow passengers that you're upset "the pilot wasn't at our regular AA meeting last night."

• Argue with the flight attendant, saying that a "bracing position" probably works fine when someone's Volvo station wagon hits your Toyota sedan at twenty miles per hour, but the sudden interruption of your flight by a mountaintop is likely to make such precautions futile.

- Tell a fellow passenger that you're certainly willing to put out your cigarette if he'll let you use his ear as an ashtray.

- Sell ID bracelets to fellow passengers to make it easier for their next of kin to claim their bodies "in case you-know-what happens."

Amway Parties

Obviously, Will Rogers never met an Amway salesperson. But you've certainly had the pleasure, and your next Amway presentation will be even more pleasurable if you come prepared with these monstrously impudent things to say.

- Say to your Amway party host, "Mind coming? What makes you think that I object to being lured to your home under the false pretense that you're having a party and subjected to an incredibly intense hard sell to buy ten cases of some totally useless household cleaner for an outrageously exorbitant price?"

- Agree that you'll buy several dozen gallons of imitation maple syrup if your distributor will stand on his head in the middle of Interstate 90 playing a kazoo and sending SOS signals with his legs.

- Graciously decline the invitation to have a distributor "sponsor you," pointing out that as you see it, such a relationship is very similar to the one that usually exists between pimps and prostitutes.

4

• Ask how many friends, acquaintances, and relatives you have to betray and ultimately sell down the river in order to make your monthly sales quota.

• Inquire when the company plans to branch out into more exotic products such as outhouse furniture, do-it-yourself embalming kits, and a granola-type snack bar made from camel dung.

• In order to determine the exact number of salesmen still in your territory, ask whether or not dead distributors are considered "inactive."

Animal Rights Protests and "Save the Earth" Demonstrations

Don't let those party-pooping do-gooders spoil your gutting, skinning, and tanning fun. Strike back by deploying these gruesomely churlish things to say and do at your next protest meeting.

• Ask if "Save the Whales" means that from now on Roseanne Arnold will be on the endangered species list.

• Solicit money for a "Pave the Brazilian Rain Forest" campaign.

• Walk up to Bob Barker and tell him you're an avid vivisectionist.

• Pick up a megaphone and announce that since protesters would prefer to have painful gene research done on people rather than animals, you're willing to "donate several activists right now."

• Open a concession stand to sell acid raincoats.

- Launch a "No Hypocrites" counterprotest and throw cheeseburgers, suede skirts, and leather belts at the other demonstrators.

- Taunt protesters by shouting, "Over 80 billion served!"

- Campaign to "recycle Rosemary Clooney" and get two new people out of her.

- Tell protest organizers that the only kind of dragnet you're interested in is the one starring Sergeant Joe Friday.

- Write and distribute a book entitled *Fifty More Things You Can Do to Destroy the Earth.*

Annual Physicals

Nothing gives you greater peace of mind than a comprehensive yearly checkup ending with a "clean bill of health." To help ensure that your annual visits are in fact memorable, review these brutishly low things to do and say during your next exam.

- When checking in with the receptionist, offer comments such as: "Nice waiting room. Could you make it any smaller, and could you overbook it any more, and could you keep us all standing any longer in a small, airless room filled with a pathetic collection of whining, wheezing, misbegotten hypochondriacs?"

- Pretend you're from the fire department and ask to see the occupancy permit for the waiting room.

- Tell people in the waiting room that you're a pharmaceutical company representative and that you'd be happy to sell them samples out of the trunk of your car.

• Announce that you're an inspector with the state health department and that you've got something urgent to discuss with the doctor about the results of his or her recent blood screening test.

• Wear a gauze mask and a sign that says WARNING: CONTAGIOUS.

• Leave in the waiting room a stack of postcards addressed to your state's congressmen signed, "another fed-up consumer in favor of socialized medicine."

• When the nurse goes to take a blood sample and says it will "only be a little prick," unzip your fly and say "Wanna bet?"

Apartment Rentals

Get out that magnifying glass and be sure to read the small print in your lease. When you're done, practice saying and doing these abominably vulgar things while renting (or being evicted from) your next apartment or house.

• Ask the rental agent if vermin come with the apartment or if you have to supply your own.

• During an initial tour of the apartment complex, remark that it would be "a great place for a devil worshiping shrine."

• Ask if you can put down your spouse's gold tooth for the security deposit.

• Remind the rental agent that the major kitchen appliances were "probably cleaned last about the same time they stopped making Studebakers."

• Ask the landlord if there's a separate utility charge for your coal oven, gas lanterns, rocks to wash clothes on, etc.

- Once you've moved in, insist on repainting the entire apartment black, noting that "white is so depressing."

- Introduce your snarling bull mastiff to the landlord, saying, "Don't worry, he's out of quarantine now and I think he's got that rabies thing licked!"

- Tell the landlord you assume it's OK to operate a home-based business such as a call-girl network, drug ring, IRA bomb factory, drug addict's shooting gallery, or Mafia safe house.

- When complaining about the lack of heat in your unit, ask the landlord, "Exactly how many mice are driving that turbine?"

- If the neighbor's children are bothering you, bring them into your apartment, demonstrate how the trash compactor works and suggest that they take turns playing house inside it.

Autopsies

Autopsies offer a special challenge to rude people because almost everyone is overdressed, it's awfully cold, and the coroner's power saw makes a kind of high-speed drone that sounds remarkably like a chainsaw cutting through a hind quarter. You'll fit right in if you do and say these boorishly repugnant things at a postmortem examination.

• Have tickets printed up with the date, place, and time of the autopsy, and then try to scalp them outside the morgue.

• Open a concession stand to sell barf bags, rubber boots, smelling salts, etc.

• Bring in a video camcorder so that you can make tapes, pointing out that "Geraldo will pay big bucks for this."

• Ask the medical examiner if you can make a connect-the-dots puzzle when she's done.

- Insist on bringing in a boom box and playing these rock classics:

  "Wake Me, Shake Me"

  "Another One Bites the Dust"

  "Cuts Like a Knife"

  "Biggest Part of Me"

  "Bits and Pieces"

  "Don't Leave Me This Way"

- Stop the medical examiner when he reaches for the scalpel and say urgently, "Wait a minute—I think I saw her hand move!"

- Just as the pathologist completes the Y-shaped incision, say, "Remember that part in *Alien* where the guy starts choking and . . ."

- About twenty minutes into the procedure, loudly suggest that "everyone's probably hungry and we should send out for cold cuts."

- Take bets on how much the viscera will weigh.

- Interrupt an inspection of the stomach contents by saying, "Darn, I'm famished! Who's up for pizza?"

- Offer to referee a game where contestants on each side of the examining table take turns trying to toss the vital organs back into the proper cavity.

- When the autopsy is almost completed, yell out, "Hey, look at this! This toe tag says *George* Smith, not John Smith!"

- Upon completion of the examination, tell the pathologist that you need "a doggie bag for the table scraps."

Bail Hearings

"Eye-opening" is the best way to describe a tour through this side street of the criminal justice system. So, warm up your voice box and reach deep into your wallet as you say and do these horrendously indecorous things at your next bail hearing.

• Attend the hearing with a lawyer dressed as the Angel of Death.

• Wear a shirt with a large arrow on the back pointing to the prosecutor that says I'M ONLY HERE BECAUSE SOME IDIOT BAR EXAMINER FELT SORRY AND GAVE THIS NITWIT ENOUGH POINTS TO PASS THE TEST.

• When the judge asks if a "stenographic record is requested," say, "No, I'd much prefer either a CD or a laser disc."

• Convince the judge that the police really have arrested the wrong person with this fail-safe explanation: "Judge, they ain't got no case. I picked up the wrong suitcase is all. It looked just like mine, but it hadda Uzi, some funny money, and some nonprescription drugs, that kinda thing. It was like a mistaken identity. I'm just a travelin' salesman. I swear, by the time they schedule a trial, they won't even have no witnesses. They'll be, you know, incommunicado— you know, that Latin thing where they ain't gonna talk unless you torture them with hot coals or threaten to shoot a relative in the face. If you was to ask me, I'd say, I think by then they'll have left town. So, Judge, I wouldn't be worryin' about my showin' up for no trial that ain't gonna happen in the first place, and even if it did I wasn't gonna get convicted anyways."

- Ask the judge, "Who starts your car for you in the morning?"

- Explain that your two cousins, Angelo and Tiny, "just as a courtesy," have repeatedly inquired about the health of the judge and her family.

- Tell the judge that you admire the fine job he's doing, that you know how poorly civil servants get paid, and that he deserves a bonus. Then hand him a blank check and ask him to fill it in.

- In a murder case, argue that you should be allowed out on bail because you "don't see the victim down here complaining about it."

- When objecting to the judge's bail decision, make sure to

    1. appeal to the state supreme court;

16

2. deliver a suspicious-looking package to the courthouse; and

3. sell stag films showing the judge and a pony named Pixie cavorting at the old Mustang Ranch in Las Vegas.

• When requesting bail on a murder charge, use these time-tested "can't miss" arguments:

1. "I was cleanin' my gun and it went off and hit the guy three, maybe four times at most."

2. "I was makin' an ice sculpture for a picnic, and this guy just slipped on a nearby walkway and impaled himself on the end of my ice pick."

3. "This ain't no murder. He was competin' in one of those marathons or somethin'. He was trainin'. You know how they train with weights on their ankles and wrists. Well he couldn't afford no expensive ones, so he was wearin' these cement sneakers and then he goes and trips and falls in the river, and one thing leads to another and he drowns."

4. "No, it was a freak accident. Happens all the time at construction sites. He wasn't watchin' where he was goin' and all of a sudden he goes and falls off a steel girder about four hundred feet up. Then the other guys in the crew are workin' real hard and they don't notice him and they go and knock a

17

form together and pour cement for a couple of days, and the next thing you know he's part of a thirty-story apartment buildin'."

• Tell the judge that you won't even consider pre-trial detainment in the county jail unless you are promised "a very extensive continental menu, complete with a wide variety of fine French wines, gourmet dinner entrees, and an innovative program of live entertainment."

• Suggest that the judge herself hold the bail money because it would make you feel a lot better and maybe "if all the money isn't there later on it wouldn't be a problem."

• Have your bondsman post the bail in Mexican pesos.

• Argue for personal recognizance, pointing out that you never failed to show up for trial on the fourteen previous murder charges brought against you.

• Suggest to the judge that, in lieu of cash, you'd like to put up as bail the drug shipment you're expecting from Colombia. If that doesn't work, ask to substitute any of the following: your time-share in the PTL Club's Religious Ranch, an IRA in the Silverado Savings & Loan, some junk bonds issued by the DeLorean Car Company, or a personal promissory note signed by Michael Milken.

Barhopping

First things first. Get your head out of the toilet long enough to post bond. Then make sure you've had several more drinks before practicing these disgracefully vile things to say and do during your next drinking contest and barroom brawl.

- Ask Kitty Dukakis to appear in the lounge to help attract new business.

- Before you commence throwing chairs or hitting other customers with broken bottles, introduce yourself and the other members of your drinking party.

- Organize a party to salute the National Woman's Temperance Union.

- Play a new bar game called Cookie Toss, during which drunken customers vomit for both distance and accuracy.

- Schedule an Unhappy Hour, when whining, crying, kvetching people get up on stage and sob into the microphone about who has more problems.

• Sponsor a Mr. Barfly or a Ms. Lounge Lizard contest.

• Offer your services as a bartender and insist on putting a real rusty nail in a rusty nail cocktail.

• Ask Betty Ford if you can put a "small saloon" in her treatment center.

• Organize an "outing" party, where bar regulars are enticed to reveal the last names of alcoholics they met at an AA meeting.

• Hold an Assholes Only Night, where the week's worst jerk must sit on a barstool and be pelted by garbage, beer cans, and diseased and partially calcified livers.

• Seize control of the karaoke machine and warble Barry Manilow songs until everyone agrees to pick up your tab.

Barbecues, Luaus, and Picnics

Barbecues, luaus, and picnics offer a welcome chance to favorably influence friends, neighbors, and relatives. Just dust off the grill and try saying and doing these unconscionably inconsiderate things.

• If the invitation is limited to you and your immediate family, be sure to bring several neighbors, their children, and in-laws.

• Offer to tend bar and in a boisterous and condescending voice announce, "Hey, I think these people deserve the good stuff. I know you've got it here someplace!"

• While cooking, if you accidentally drop some meat on the ground, don't hesitate to pick it up and throw it back on the grill while assuring everyone, "Don't worry. I caught it on the first bounce."

• Add extra zest to the salad by mixing in a handful of rose bugs.

- Immediately after preparing, cooking, or handling any food product, offer a blanket apology for having forgotten to "wash that pesticide off my hands."

- Go up to a particularly stout diner and say, "I haven't been keeping an exact count, but isn't that your thirteenth hot dog?"

- Ask the host if your children can "urinate in the pool, since it's chlorinated."

- When all of the cleanup work is done, offer the assistance of your spouse and children.

- Before leaving for the evening, hijack a large, expensive cooler and empty the refrigerator of any remaining beer, wine, steak, cheese, or other quality food and drink.

Beach Parties

You'll have a bitchin' bad day catchin' a ray when you employ these egregiously shabby things to say and do at your next beach party.

- Paint your kite to look like a kamikaze plane and have it dive-bomb bothersome sunbathers.

- Sell PAM as a sun block.

- Find music that's universally annoying, such as polka hits or tunes of the Australian outback, and turn the volume dial of your boom box up to 8.9.

- Put insulting notes in bottles and drop them in the ocean.

- Find a ninety-eight-pound weakling and kick sand in his face.

- Ask to borrow someone else's towel to use as a diaper because you're "saving the good ones for the ride home."

- Find a big private home with a long entranceway

and then sell all-day parking passes at ten dollars a pop to the first twenty or thirty cars you can jam in the driveway.

- Invite total strangers to change their clothes at your neighbor's condo.

- Just to entertain the lifeguard, pretend you and your group of twenty-six sun-baked friends are drowning, one after the other.

- When someone nearby falls asleep, bury her in sand up to her neck, and then as the tide starts to come in offer to dig her out for the right price.

- Create a properly romantic beach scene by having two extremely agile friends cover themselves with a greasy oil until they glisten and then grope one another in a loud, vulgar display of sexual acrobatics.

- Launch a Don't Gross Us Out Contest to find the most disgusting body in a bathing suit.

- Set up an aluminum reflector device to divert extremely concentrated bursts of solar light onto fellow bathers' noses, ears, feet, and buttocks.

- Yell "Shark!" every fifteen or twenty minutes to clear out the water so you can swim in peace.

- Get out your metal detector and pretend it makes a clicking noise whenever you pass over someone's head.

- Before leaving for the day, collect all your trash and stuff it into someone else's beer cooler.

Cab Rides

Unforgettable cab rides deserve unforgettable responses—so memorize these screechingly bestial things to say during your next trip.

- If another prospective fare asks you whether or not you'd mind sharing the cab, respond by saying, "No, not if you don't mind being assaulted."

- Ask the driver if Reagan was still president the last time the cab was cleaned.

- Remind your full-bearded driver that "facial hair is a great nesting area for lice, mites, and other forms of vermin."

- Inquire of the driver, "What genus of fungus is growing on the back floor and arm rest?"

- Suggest that "the taximeter was probably certified for accuracy by the same people who designed the O rings for the *Challenger* shuttle launch."

- If the driver is stopped at a red light and is about

to take a bite of his sandwich, ask, "Who blew lunch in this ashtray?"

• Inquire about how much of your cab fare is being funneled to fundamentalist terrorist groups.

• Advise the driver that she missed at least one pothole and suggest that she "drive around the block, and get it right this time!"

• Warn your driver that it took thirteen zombies just to wash down three Tex-Mex combo dinners, but if he wants to keep racing from traffic light to traffic light and jamming on his brakes, that's OK with you.

• Ask who passed the cab for inspection, noting that you also have a car with bald tires, cracked windows, no door handles, two missing headlights, and a foot-long hole in the rear floorboard, and you need a sticker too.

• On a twelve-dollar cab ride, give the driver a ten-dollar bill and say, "Keep the change."

• Pull out a gun and pretend it's a holdup.

• Admire the driver's photo ID, saying it looks remarkably similar to the child molester you saw featured on "America's Most Wanted."

• When you arrive at your destination, tell the cabbie that you're sorry but you must have left your wallet in your other pants.

Car Dealerships and Repair Shops

You love 'em. You hate 'em. But you can't live without 'em. So make the best of it and use these mortifyingly petulant things to say and do the next time you visit.

• Ask a Japanese car dealer if you can get a special rebate because it's the anniversary of "our dropping the big one on Hiroshima."

• Tell the salesperson that he's welcome to accompany you on your test drive provided he can "hang onto the rear bumper at high speed."

• Ask if the dealership is at present under indictment for any major felony.

• Inquire whether the trunk's large enough so that your in-laws will fit comfortably.

• Visit a Renault or Peugeot dealer, snap the dealer's suspenders, yank his waxed moustache, and remind him that the last time a French car won the Le

Mans Grand Prix the Nazi flag was flying over the Eiffel Tower.

- Picket the dealership, handing out plastic lemons with the car dealer's name on it.

- Remind the dealer that *"Consumer Reports* has given this car more blackballs than Lee Elder got when he applied for membership at the Pebble Beach Golf Club."

- Tell the salesperson that your brand-new car is making exactly the same high-pitched whine that *he* made the week before when he was trying to sell it to you.

- Suggest to the mechanic that because the car has been recalled so many times, "Wouldn't it be a lot easier if you would just call me and tell me what days during the month I can actually drive the car?"

- Warn the mechanic that you came to the dealership "for a tune-up, not a holdup."

- Advise the service manager that both his front and rear end will be out of alignment if he doesn't fix your shimmy soon.

College Admission Interviews

Drinking contests. Fraternity parties. Senior-year blowouts. All this and more will be yours only if you put into practice these incredibly wretched things to say and do during your college admission interviews.

• Explain that your high school grades would have been a lot better if you hadn't been caught cheating so many times.

• Demand to help defray the cost of tuition by performing sexual acts with the dean's wife.

• Inquire whether they're "really serious" about trying to collect on student loans.

• During your Appalachian State interview, display a .22-caliber rifle and several skinned animal pelts, pointing out that "varmints are good eatin'."

• When attempting to gain admission to a southern college, you can enhance your prospects by

　　1. wearing a blue Army of the Republic uniform;

29

2. reminding the interviewer that "Lee got his ass kicked good and proper, didn't he?";

3. inquiring if college officials and the general student body still beat black students;

4. asking whether Klan members have their own dorm; and

5. calling the interviewer "Colonel."

• Offer to prepay for all the anticipated damage to college property you plan to cause.

• Ask if you'll actually have to attend classes, write papers, take exams, and do research to pass your courses.

• Make sure college officials are apprised of other strong points favoring your early admission:

1. You took the SAT.

2. You scored in the upper 85 percent on the annual ringworm identification exam.

3. You really like the campus.

4. Your parents earn in the six figures.

5. You're able to swim the sidestroke on either side.

6. You'll probably drop at least five thousand bucks at the student union.

• Don't be afraid to ask questions at the interview. For example:

> **1.** How many incompletes and withdrawals can I get each semester?
>
> **2.** Can I buy an all-you-can-drink beer pass for the year?
>
> **3.** Is the library strict about returning stolen books and mutilated magazines?

Dale Carnegie Courses

Win friends? Doubtful. Influence others? Maybe, but probably not in the way the instructors intend when you say and do these despicably insolent things at a Dale Carnegie course.

• Explain to instructors that "it's hard to be friends with people who charge so much money for such a short course."

• Announce that you haven't seen Dale recently and ask if he's being tortured in a back room until he "pretends to like Richard Nixon."

• Ask if you'll be entitled to a rebate if you continue to get bags of hate mail from people you've barely met.

• Offer to perform blood tests on all course instructors to determine the chemical stimulant responsible for their abnormal perkiness.

• Insist that the instructor name three things that she likes about Saddam Hussein.

- Point out to the lecturer that the last time you encountered someone with such a frozen smile and backslapping friendliness, he was being invited to the operating room for a full frontal lobotomy.

- Help out the instructor by recommending four new ways to get people to sit up and pay attention when you walk in the room:

> **1.** Pretend you have a split personality and have one side of your mouth argue with the other side.

> **2.** Bring in a pet turtle, coax it gently out of its shell, and then bite its head off.

> **3.** Place a lighted cigarette in your left ear, inhale deeply, and then pinch your nostrils and try blowing so hard that the smoke goes out your right ear.

> **4.** When someone recites the old biblical injunction "let he among you who has not sinned cast the first stone," reply, "OK" and grab the biggest boulder you can find and throw it at his head.

Dave Del Dotto
Real Estate Seminars

Do your homework and you too can laugh all the way to the bank. Prepare for sudden fame and fortune by rehearsing these venomously foul things to say and do at your next real estate seminar.

- Ask Dave why Tom Vu "gets all the babes."

- Offer to come on his program and help him sell a certain concrete and steel suspension bridge that is now connecting the boroughs of Manhattan and Brooklyn.

- Inquire whether his "cash flow" system is really a one-way-only stream, with the cash flowing straight into his pockets.

- Inform Dave that the last time you went to a bank and asked to borrow money to buy income-producing property "with no money down," the loan officer asked a nearby psychiatric clinic to examine your head.

- Suggest to Dave that he bears an uncanny resemblance to Boxcar Willie.

- Quietly advise John Davidson that he's beginning to remind you of a "carnival barker out at the old fairgrounds."

- Spread a rumor that Tony Robbins's profit margins are bigger than Dave's.

- Remind Dave that his sales technique appears disturbingly similar to that used by the "bad mice" to break the willpower of Mighty Mouse's girlfriend.

- Take the microphone away from John Davidson, strike him repeatedly about the head and shoulders, and announce that although you've followed Dave's advice and bought up a lot of property at dirt cheap prices near Love Canal, Three Mile Island, and the San Andreas Fault line, you can't seem to unload it on another buyer.

- Offer the following as titles for Dave's next bestsellers:

Nine Ways to Make Me Money

Nearer Thy Gold to Me

My Hand in Thy Pocket

Deb Balls

Debutante balls have outdone themselves by reaching the apex of stuffy, cloying pretension and no-holds-barred social climbing. You'll be sure to fit right in at the next ball when you employ these grievously gauche things to say and do.

• Apologize for your date's absence by pointing out that "she's in the ladies room readjusting the safety pin in her nose and having a toot."

• Suggest to one of your female table companions that you "remember seeing her at the Harlem Cotillion, waiting on tables."

• Invite a society matron to dance. While no one is looking, silently unzip your trousers, stop in the middle of the dance floor, and then push her away while screaming at the top of your lungs, "For God's sake, Mrs. Van Cleef, you're old enough to be my mother! Can't you keep your hands outta my pants for even one minute!"

- Go from table to table looking for a girl named "Babs" or "Muffy." Once located, pass her a telegram that states, URGENT NOTICE—CENTER FOR DISEASE CONTROL—ATLANTA, GEORGIA, CALL 1-800-REAL-SIK.

- Ask people at your table, "Has anyone here seen my Spanish fly? I left it here a minute ago."

- When people inquire about your family pedigree, tell them that your father's a Mafia soldier, pimp, and drug dealer and your mother's a topless dancer and prostitute.

- Tell everyone in the receiving line that "Chip and his friends are abusing themselves in the men's rest room."

- Promise one of the debs at the bar that you can get her boyfriend a job at a posh country club because you know they're now "hiring Filipino workers."

- Inform one of your tablemates that you're sure you remember seeing him at the gay leather bar in SoHo.

- Apologize for your late arrival but point out that you "got held up at the nude lounge."

- Go to the receiving line, identify yourself as William K. Smith, and invite all the women to join you and Uncle Ted for drinks later.

Dental Appointments

Fed up with the frequent indignities and inconvenience of modern dental treatment? Now you can fight back with these proven sensibility-numbing suggestions for your next visit.

- Wear a T-shirt that says, I LIKE DENTISTS . . . TIED TO A 200-LB. TEST LINE AND USED FOR CHUM WHEN I GO GREAT WHITE SHARK FISHING.

- While in the reception area, circulate Amnesty International's toll-free torture-report number.

- Amuse children in the waiting room by telling them stories about Dr. Dan, the perverted dental vampire who likes to molest cavity-prone children by drilling two little holes in their necks and sucking out their gums.

- When filling out the new patient information sheet, emphasize the fact that your brother's an attorney who specializes in dental malpractice.

• Tell the hygienist that you wouldn't need a broad-spectrum antibiotic if she "washed her hands once in a while."

• As you pass by each treatment room, compare your abscessing gums, oral lesions, herpes infections, and ulcerating cankers with other patients'.

• Ask the bookkeeper how many cc's of nitrous oxide she inhaled before preparing your bill.

• Tell the doctor you are an OSHA undercover agent and you want to see her "hepatitis B compliance forms."

• Tell the dentist that you enjoy coming there about as much as you like

> **1.** sticking your face in a pot of boiling hydrochloric acid;
>
> **2.** stepping on a plank filled with barbed nails; or
>
> **3.** getting your arthritic fingers crushed in a swinging meat-locker door.

• Complain that the grinding noise from the dental drill is too low and that they should take the muffler off and "use the foot pedal to rev it up nice and loud."

• Give the dentist a quick endodontic quiz by asking him to pick which of the following is a positive indication for apical surgery:

1. useless, expensive, and vexatious treatments are usually covered by the patient's dental plan;

2. the patient wants an itemized statement and recently objected to a triple overbilling; or

3. the dentist's wife needs a new Rolex diamond watch.

• Ask if it's normal for your silver amalgam fillings to be picking up short-wave radio broadcasts from Singapore.

Diet Support Groups

More conscious than ever of body image, Americans have been flocking to diet centers like maggots to the rotting corpse of the Ayatollah Khomeini. As a result, you can have a lot of fun by saying and doing these unbearably uncivil things at your next diet group meeting.

• Advise the group leader that you appreciate a realistic weight loss challenge; e.g., one pound every three years.

• Suggest that "these blimps" could quickly learn a little weight control if "they just stopped using those toy shovels to eat with."

• Ask a particularly fat person, "Who reads the scale for you?"

• Tell the group members you're a famous Hollywood movie producer and you're "looking for a stunt double for Marlon Brando."

- Initiate a Rolling Layers of Humongous Blubber Competition.

- If someone recommends "role playing" to aid weight loss, insist on playing the part of the dinner roll.

- Inquire whether group member Bertha's special exercise program consists of anything other than speed-walking from the refrigerator to the microwave to the oven to the dining room table.

- Tell Bob the Blob that normally you'd recommend one-on-one counseling but that he's so fat "it would have to be one-on-three counseling."

- Announce that you've got truffles in your backyard and "everyone's invited to come over and put their snouts to good use."

- Tell the woman standing next to you that you've "never seen a skin-tight tent dress before."

Dirty Movies

Traci Lords. John Holmes. Vanessa Del Rio. What a lineup. You'll be able to hit for both average and power when you pound out these noxiously offensive things to do on your next visit to the dirty movies.

• Kick the seat of the guy in front of you and proclaim loudly, "Hey, if you're gonna do that, at least have the decency to do it in the men's room."

• Walk around the movie theater wearing a raincoat with a sign that says 25 CENTS FOR ONE PEEK, 3 FOR A QUARTER.

• Tell the usher that you think that "coming attractions" is spelled incorrectly.

• Walk around the lobby and practice heavy breathing sounds.

• Have a friend call the movie theater and ask them to page Pee Wee Herman.

Divorce Trials

Parting is such sweet sorrow. You'll be able to speed up the healing process immeasurably when you take these unrelentingly uncouth suggestions.

- Paint a bull's-eye on the back of your ex-husband's attorney.

- During live testimony, start a loud, involved argument about who gets to keep the solar-driven sexual appliances.

- Insist that you're willing to send alimony payments to your wife only if she stops having group sex with car salesmen on the front lawn of your former home.

- When you prepare a schedule of the personal property you want out of the divorce, be sure to list your ex's colon and spleen.

- Hire a private investigator to testify that he has pictures of your wife in bed with a trumpet, a clarinet, and bagpipes, "and it's not pretty."

- Tell the judge that since your wife consummated the marriage with a drunken baggage porter while you were paying the cab driver, you think that all you really need is an annulment, not a divorce.

- Make your first alimony payment by filling a wheelbarrow with thousands of Canadian pennies.

- Tell the court that since no agreement can be reached on who gets the dog, Rover should be brought to a vet, and forcibly bisected and the rear end awarded to your husband.

- Demand a divorce on grounds that your wife is a Nu Skin distributor.

- Tell the judge that everything was going along OK until your husband decided to become a Mormon and marry your best friend, a cowgirl, and several other women he had known for at least a week.

- Belittle the other attorney by repeatedly referring to him as "a boot-licking stooge," "a pinheaded bully," or simply "that clown in the K mart suit."

- Accuse your wife of now trying to do to you in a courtroom what she's refused to do to you in the bedroom for the past three years.

- Explain that you first became suspicious of your wife's fidelity when she said that Jack Kennedy was a good friend of hers.

- The day before your final divorce hearing, pretend you're calling from the clerk of court's office and send your husband's divorce lawyer on a wild-goose chase to a bogus hearing in a county on the other side of the state.

• Insist on having your wife's blood tested and crossmatched against "any male within three hundred miles of her during the time period when she became pregnant."

Drive-by Shootings

Ready . . . Aim . . . Duck! You'll have to practice all three steps while taking these nefariously outrageous actions during your next drive-by shooting.

- Wear a jeans patch that says "Don't shoot me, I'm not a gang member."

- Insist on "posing" for a shooting, pointing out you get "shot best from the left side."

- Sell Street Gang Trading Cards that feature front and side view photos of gang members taken from police station mug shots.

- Recommend that gang members try to reduce the growing number of innocent deaths and injuries by asking them to wear lemon-yellow vests with the word TARGET emblazoned on the back.

- Ask movie theater operators to schedule showings of films like *New Jack City* and *Boyz N the Hood* at the same time so that members will get out simultaneously and be able to start shooting without wasting a lot of time.

• Tax the gangs for strictly random shootings.

• Encourage gun companies to offer lucrative endorsement contracts to gang members who appear in commercials touting the advantages of using a particular handgun, automatic weapon, or rocket launcher.

• Sell maps of popular Hollywood shooting spots and offer lead bulletproof bus tours for out-of-towners who want to videotape live shootouts.

• Open concession stands in gang-ridden neighborhoods to sell film, bandages, ammo clips, organ transplant cards, burial insurance, and other useful products.

• Suggest that Universal Studios offer a new tour ride called "Mausoleum Land," during which passengers are forced to take a ride through East L.A. in a chopped and channeled 1951 Mercury coupe while mechanical robots take turns popping up from rooftops, garbage cans, and other cars to shoot high-velocity hollow points at them.

Drug Busts

You have the right to remain silent. You have the right to have an attorney present during questioning. And you're gonna need both those rights after putting these scurrilously grating suggestions into practice during your next drug bust.

- Wear a T-shirt that says "STONED AGAIN."

- When the cop starts frisking you, tell him that it feels good but you'd like it "a little bit farther to the left and with a lot more feeling."

- Whatever the cop says, yell, "Entrapment!"

- Explain that you're a pharmacist making a late-night home delivery.

- Explain to the policeman that the Miranda rights are based on an old 1940s movie starring Carmen Miranda, and when he reads you your rights he must wear a headdress made of fake oranges, bananas, and grapefruit.

• As soon as a cop tries to interrogate you, slip a wad of ten- and twenty-dollar bills into his pocket and yell loudly, "Don't worry, captain, I've got your bribe right here!"

• When asked about a Colombian connection, respond by admitting that although you've seen the TV commercial, you're still pretty confused about which is the freshly ground and which is the freeze-dried.

• Advise the police to be nice to you because your brother-in-law's "across the street getting all this on videotape."

• If a detective tells you that you fit the profile of a drug courier, tell him he fits the profile of someone who's taken too many blows to the head.

• If asked to "answer a few questions at the station," tell the police you're gonna follow Nancy Reagan's advice and "just say no."

• Insist that you don't know what happened—that you were thirsty and ordered a Coke, and all of a sudden you got busted.

• Demand to use your drug stash instead of cash when posting bail.

• Point out that you would probably remember if you had recently inserted a contraband object in your rectum, but the cops are free to take a look if they'd like.

Drug Buys

Tired of having to "just say no"? Try a few of these remarks instead—they're guaranteed to make your next drug score a truly hallucinatory experience.

• Ask if the drugs come with a thirty-day warranty and make sure the dealer explains his return policy.

• Warn the dealer that any bait-and-switch tactics will be immediately reported to the Consumer Protection Agency.

• Explain that since you haven't "had a chance to cash those stolen payroll checks," you'd like to put the coke on layaway.

• Tell the drug dealer that you believe his attempts to gain control of the "entire corner" are in violation of the Sherman Anti-Trust Act.

Earthquake Drills

Going, going, gone! By the year 2000, thousands of Californians will personally experience the upper end of the Richter scale. You'll be ready for the big one if you practice these unnervingly repulsive comments and actions during your next earthquake drill.

- Tell people to "wear something comfortable" because it will take rescue workers several days, if not weeks, to locate them.

- Suggest drama therapy where people go on stage and pretend to be the buildings that will be flattened when the TransAmerica pyramid "gets horizontal."

- Insist that all drill participants begin screaming in agony "just for practice."

- Rehearse valuable postquake survival techniques such as fainting, moaning, and looting.

- Recommend that everyone purchase a seeing-eye dog and white cane so that "they can practice getting around after being blinded by flying shards of razor-sharp glass."

• Practice limbo dancing in preparation for trying to walk underneath collapsed furniture, flattened doorways, and pancaked porches.

• Make an announcement that you're a certified emergency medical technician and you intend to auction your services to the highest bidder.

• Tell especially fat people that the rest of the group wants to "hide under them during the simulation."

• Find your ass, grab it firmly with both hands, and kiss it goodbye.

Elevator Rides

Elevator rides play on the common fears of towering heights, enclosed spaces, and breathtaking speed. Employing these blatantly diabolical deeds and remarks during your next elevator ride is sure to bring the phobia level of your fellow passengers to a new high.

• When you reach a particular floor, keep one foot in the elevator and put one foot out and have a debate with yourself about whether to stay or go.

• Closely examine the elevator inspection certificate and announce to fellow passengers, "Look! This thing hasn't been inspected since 1981!"

• No matter where the elevator is about to stop, yell out, "This is my floor!" Then remain motionless when the elevator stops.

• Lean over to the person next to you and say, "Excuse me, but do you *normally* use a deodorant?

• Ask fellow occupants if they've ever seen *The Towering Inferno*.

• Say to a nearby passenger, "Excuse me, but I would appreciate it if you kept your hand in your own pocket. We just met."

• Inquire, "Is it my imagination or is that a rat chewing on the emergency telephone cord?"

• Press the emergency stop button and, after stumbling groggily to your feet, announce that you always wanted to "see if that thing worked."

• Accuse anyone wearing a trench coat of being "the flasher they're looking for on the second floor."

• Dress up as an elevator operator and then push people out the door while saying, "This is your floor—get off!"

• When passengers carrying large packages are attempting to board the elevator, see how many times you can hit the "close door" button before they angrily retrieve their squashed boxes and agree to wait for the next elevator.

• Openly fondle and grope your date but then stop and holler, "Not here! There's no outlet for Mr. Weenie Wand!"

• Suddenly and without warning, turn off the light switch while stating, "Damn, I knew we shouldn't have fired the maintenance super!"

• When a particularly obese person attempts to enter the elevator, press the "close door" button and explain that "the freight elevator is just down the hallway to your left."

- Ask the man behind you, "Have you seen my colostomy bag? I know I had it when I got on."

- Hit the button for every floor of a twenty-four-story building and then get off on the second floor.

Graceland Tours

What could be more fun than glorying in these contemptuously lurid things to say and do while checking out the King (or what's left of him) at his Kingdom in Memphis?

• Suggest that a Burger King be opened on the grounds.

• Ask the tour guide, "When can I see the body?"

• Ask to see Elvis's blue suede shoes so you can step on them.

• Ask if it's true that Elvis could burp, fart, cough, snort, sneeze, and hiccup at the same time, but he did it only once and it killed him.

• Offer bourbon, beer, and munchies to your fellow tourists and then ask for a moment of silence so that you can all "cut wind" in memory of the King.

• Ask for the real lowdown on "that paternity suit involving the martian woman."

- As a personal tribute to the King, shoot out every television in the rec room.

- Wear a button that says I THINK HE BOUGHT IT BUT I'M STILL HOPIN'.

Hair-Loss Clinics

Hair loss can be caused by age, sex, racial discrimination, stress, even premature ejaculation. But don't worry. Once you've mastered these ruthlessly crass things to say and do the next time you find yourself at a hair-loss clinic, everyone *else*'s hair will start falling out.

• Slap a five-dollar bill on the counter and ask for "the hair of the dog that bit me."

• Dress up as a police officer and tell the clinic owner that you have a "warrant for whoever stole Sinead O'Connor's hair" and they'd "better come quietly."

• Inquire about the combination package that includes 20 percent more hair and a really deep, masculine-sounding voice.

• Ask about the entry-level "cue-ball cure," which consists of a technician painting hair on a bald head with a brown Magic Marker.

• When a male friend admits to being a clinic client, check his veracity by grabbing a handful of hair and giving it a playful tug.

• Ask to meet the black man in the television commercial who in the "before" photo looks like a wire terrier and in the "after" photo looks like Buckwheat.

• When ordering your human hair weave, be sure to ask the technician to "hold the lice."

• Order "a side of dandruff with a touch of psoriasis" to add a touch of realism to your hair transplant.

• Tell the salesperson that you appreciate the fact that he'll "stand behind the product" but you want to know exactly how many hundreds of miles behind that might be.

• Ask the hair technician, "Is this the same topical solution that grew hair on rats but also gave them tumors the size of the state of Rhode Island?"

• Complain bitterly that your toupee looks so artificial that your friends have been calling you "Du Pont Stainmaster" and "Wall to Wall."

• Tell them that you understand that "the gradual hair replacement" system is a five-step process: first, they examine the color of your money; second, they rinse the big bills out of your wallet; third, they trim your bankroll; fourth, they blow-dry your complaints; and fifth, they cut their losses and move to the next town.

Hospital Visits

The hospital patients you're visiting will need all the sympathy they can get after you've carried out these brazenly impertinent suggestions.

• Bring in your dictionary and entertain the patient by reading aloud the definitions of such words as *asepsis, necrosis, neoplasm, sarcoma, systemic, terminal, thrombosis, toxemia,* and *virulent.*

• Encourage "regularity" in the patient by putting a mixture of liquid nitrogen and diet cola into his enema bag.

• Hire a stripper and have her strut her stuff for recent vasectomy patients.

• Keep asking if the patient has been given "the last rites."

• Coronary patients love presents. Good choices are buckets of greasy fried chicken, copies of their hospital bill, and subscriptions to *Secret Amazonian Sex Rituals* magazine.

- Ask the patient in the intensive care unit if she left anything good for you in her will.

- If you've forgotten to bring your recuperating Aunt Millie a present, borrow the flowers, balloon bouquets, and candy from the vegetating patient in the next room.

- Don't let patients get all hung up on thinking about themselves. Assure them that you've got your own share of problems that are a lot worse than theirs.

- Ask if you can borrow a patient's bedpan "for a few days."

- While her roommate is fast asleep, nudge the patient playfully and ask when her roommate "died." Then explain that you'll have to leave soon because if you stay much longer it's going to be depressing.

- Send a greeting card with a cute saying like

> Violets are blue,
> Roses are red,
> When you get this card
> I hope you're not dead.

- Explain that you've carefully checked the insurance actuary tables and found that most patients have "a one in twenty shot of beating this typically fatal disease."

Jehovah's Witnesses' Visits

What could be more fun than to be woken up on a bright, sunny Sunday morning at 7:00 A.M. by someone who wants to bring some religious enlightenment to your poor, misbegotten life? You can spread the word in your own way by following these unforgivably blasphemous suggestions the next time the folks at Kingdom Hall pay you an unsolicited visit.

- Invite your visitors in and then offer them liquor, narcotics, and promiscuous sex with your relatives.

- Agree to give them a donation if they'll make one to the Save Rosemary's Baby Foundation.

- Offer to trade a *Stoned Goths from Hell* magazine for one of their *Watchtower*s.

- Suggest that if they ever visit your home again on a Sunday before 10:00 A.M., you'll be happy to help them "meet their maker" at a time earlier than they expect.

- Ask them to stay for lunch, as you're planning a sacrificial entree of your neighbor's mongrel dog.

- When they inquire whether you know anybody who needs ministering, suggest that they call on the escaped sex offender up the street with the hair-trigger temper and rabid pit bull.

- Request the date of their annual "two-for-the-price-of-one lost souls sale."

- Ask if they've heard the joke about the lesbian mud wrestler and the Christian proselytizer.

- Tell them that if they don't get off your property right away, their next meeting will be at Kingdom come, not Kingdom Hall.

Job Interviews

Since job interviews are highly stressful for both the candidate and the interviewer, it's best to be prepared. You'll put your worst foot forward if you've memorized these detestably oppressive things to say and do at your next job interview.

• Ask if the job you're interviewing for includes the standard fringe benefits, such as employee harassment, clock docking for doctor's appointments, termination for filing workmen's comp claims, mandatory AIDS testing, forced polygraph exams, locker searches, fifteen-minute bereavement leave, and five-dollar retirement gifts.

• List as references John Gotti, Charles Manson, Michael Milken, and Imelda Marcos.

• Establish eye contact and then see if you can lure the interviewer into crossing his eyes.

• Agree to a record check if the interviewer agrees to a barium enema.

- When asked about experience, offer the details of your early sexual encounters, being careful to provide explicit details about "that bestiality charge."

- Explain that you're currently self-employed and offer a business card that states, "Will personally inspect all body orifices, $10."

- When asked what you liked best about your last job, tell your interviewer that you really enjoyed removing gum from underneath movie theater seats because you're "making a great big ball."

- When asked what you liked least about your last job, simply explain that you were "Mike Tyson's sparring partner."

- If called upon to list your strongest qualities, cite, "a really big cleft palate" and "my impressive score on the Michigan Psychopathic Inventory Profile."

- List these four things that really bother you about work in general:

    1. having to show up;

    2. having to show up on time;

    3. having to stay awake for eight consecutive hours; and

    4. having to actually do work.

- Act natural. Don't be afraid to pick your nose, scratch yourself, or clean your ears.

- Body language is crucial. Don't be afraid to wince a lot, shake your head from side to side in disagreement, hold your nose, or even flip the bird.

- Interrupt frequently and, when provoked, take off your shoe and slam it on the table for effect.

- When asked where you plan to be in five years, respond, "I hope to be seeking asylum in a warm, tropical, economically upbeat country" or "I expect I'll have received a governor's pardon by then."

- Be sure to ask these important questions:

   1. "When can I take my first personal day?"

   2. "What kind of employee theft really upsets you?"

   3. "Why is this interview taking so long, and how many days will I have to wait before I can file an improper termination or job discrimination lawsuit?"

- If asked why you want the job, say that you need the money for your drug habit or to pay for a sex-change operation or to underwrite your hobby of operating a mobile mortuary out of the back of your station wagon.

- If pressed for the reason you left your last job, offer either of these perfectly acceptable explanations:

   1. There was a definite lack of advancement opportunities for a convicted embezzler.

   2. You were so underpaid that it was hard to steal enough to make ends meet.

- Tell the interviewer you really need the job "because my probation officer is all over my ass."

Klan Rallies

A well-planned rally of Ku Klux Klan followers is sheer indulgence, as it combines all the merriment of a fancy costume party and a good old-fashioned lynching. Grab your best white sheet and pillowcase and try out these extravagantly depraved things to say and do at the next gathering.

• Offer to supply the party with necessary items such as tire irons, burlap bags, ax handles, an NAACP membership list, and an "old rugged cross."

• Sell souvenir bumper stickers that say THE INVISIBLE EMPIRE STRIKES BLACKS.

• Sign the guest book "Malcolm X."

• Bring your banjo and suggest that the band play "That Old Black Magic," "Abraham, Martin and John," "Stone Soul Picnic," "Harlem Shuffle," and the sound track of *Fiddler on the Roof*.

• Tell fellow merrymakers you have to go home early because you want to "catch Oprah's show."

- Spread the word that the Imperial Wizard's real name is Hyman Goldberg.

- Surreptitiously stick an I LOVE AL SHARPTON button on the back of the Grand Dragon's robe.

- Ask the revelers nearest you how much they were paid to appear as the "mountain folk" in the movie *Deliverance*.

- Put PAID FBI INFORMANT AND PROUD OF IT decals on the side windows of several dozen parked cars.

- Start a rumor that the sergeant at arms really likes collard greens, knishes, and chorizo.

- Offer to market a Lunatic Fringe line of trading cards, each bearing a picture of a different Klan official.

- Encourage cross burners to squirt the lighter fluid directly on the fire while holding the can with both hands.

Liberace Museum Tours

Subtle. Refined. Restrained. None of those adjectives comes within a country mile of defining the late, great Liberace. When touring his museum, tickle the ivories of fellow aficionados with these outrageously saucy antics.

- Ask why there are so many closets in the museum.

- Say to the tour guide "Gee, I thought Marc Christian would be meeting us here in his lounging pajamas! Oh, that's right, that was *Rock Hudson's* friend. I might be in the wrong place."

- While admiring a portrait of Liberace, comment that his face was nipped and tucked so much that it ended up looking like a Naugahyde sofa.

- When the tour director promises to show you Liberace's family jewels, explain, "That's not a good idea; there are women and children here!"

- Tell museum officials that you haven't seen anything "quite this tasteful and refined" since the day you were arrested in a Parisian brothel.

Mafia Conclaves

As long as you don't end up having to sleep with the fishes, consorting with mob bosses can be a lot of fun. Snap the brim of your fedora and carry out these daringly base suggestions at your next Mafia conclave.

- Promote the establishment of a Mafia Hall of Fame—and then threaten to kill anyone who suggests that it ought to be located in Cleveland.

- Recommend a Mary Kay–style distribution and profit system where points and territory are awarded on the basis of ever-increasing numbers of murders, assaults, arsons, and thefts.

- Tell John Gotti that James Brown is "real mad" at him for appropriating the name "Godfather."

- Urge that phrases like "sleeping with the fishes" and "whacked out" be replaced with "performing long-term oceanographic research" and "not accepting phone calls at this time."

- Suggest that territory be divided up in a more

71

scientific fashion, one based on the latest Nielsen ratings and other demographic information.

- Have some fun with the FBI by putting a BODY ON BOARD sign in the back window of your Lincoln Town Car.

- Make a deal with the pope whereby you sell him olive oil and wine at wholesale prices and he gives you a cut of his "indulgence sales."

- Just as the meeting is breaking up, ask if anyone "wants to go for a swim."

- Whenever the phone rings say, "Hey, Tony, it's the FBI—they've got a check for you!"

- Ask the correspondence secretary to write a letter to the big three U.S. automakers complaining that American luxury cars have been downsized so much that now "only one, or at most two, bodies will fit in the trunk."

NRA Chapter Meetings

The next time you attend a meeting of your community's local chapter of the National Rifle Association, *don't* check your gun at the door but *do* carry out these preposterously treacherous suggestions.

- Shoot first and ask questions later.

- Paste bumper stickers that read ANOTHER GAY FOR THE NRA! on members' cars.

- Hand out business cards that announce, "I'm in favor of a five-minute waiting period. Please don't kill me."

- Approach fellow meeting attendees and whisper, "Charlton Heston supported the Brady Bill! Pass it on."

- Announce an "I'll Show You Mine If You'll Show Me Yours" gun show.

- Ask if NRA members get a discount by buying their Saturday night specials on Friday night.

- Have Claudine Longet and Jean Harris conduct a hands-on pistol workshop entitled "Accidental Shootings of Unarmed Ex-Lovers."

- Wear an orange dayglow hunter's hat and put a sign on your back that says, "HEY, DUMMY—MOOSE DON'T WEAR THESE."

Near-Death Experiences

Given the fact that people seem to be inclined toward shorter, more adventurous vacations these days it's no wonder that near-death experiences are getting more and more popular. Utilize the following insufferably provocative suggestions after your next getaway.

• Explain the sensation of total peace, joy, and contentment you experienced to others by saying, "Well, you know how you would have felt if Geraldo had been hit with an even bigger chair . . ."

• Be sure to complain that in your own near-death experiences "Elvis always seems to be coming or going and the next time he abuses the system they're finally just going to let him die."

• Ask fellow returnees if they've also developed new and startling paranormal and psychic abilities, such as:

> 1. knowing that after somebody knocks a door is likely to open

2. being able to tell that a rain shower is likely to accompany black storm clouds, thunder, and lightning

3. having the uncanny ability to tell that when the phone rings, someone is trying to reach them.

• Point out that doctors have come up with a new way to shock people back to life from the brink of death: they scream in patients' ears, "Quayle got elected president! Quayle got elected president!"

Nuclear Power Plant Tours

Like it or not, nuclear power plants are here to stay. With visions of Three Mile Island and Chernobyl dancing in your head, you'll enjoy your next tour even more if you employ these glowingly nasty things to say and do.

• Shave your head, apply a generous amount of green-colored skin lotion, carry a scythe, and call yourself Mr. (or Ms.) Nuclear Fusion.

• Ask fellow tour members with you if they can "smell something burning, like a plutonium core melt-down."

• Remark loudly that the tour director reminds you of one of the hunchbacked grave robbers in *Bride of Frankenstein*.

• Threaten to borrow the fuel rods and "go fission" in the nearby creek.

• Mention that you're a former member of the Nuclear Regulatory Commission and you distinctly heard the sound of a cooling-tower operator being vaporized in the next room.

• Point out that just in your own tour group, Lucy's hair is falling out, Linda's arms are glowing in the dark, and Tom's ears blew off when he coughed.

• Ask your tour guide, "If the outside containment wall of this unit was built by brain-damaged construction workers who forgot the one-inch lead lining, what would the life expectancy of nearby inhabitants be, in milliseconds?"

• When you're asked to sign the register book, use the name "Abu Nidal," note your address as "Tripoli, Libya," and cite your occupation as "terrorist."

• Suggest a scavenger hunt during which tourists can look for cracks in the cooling tunnel pipes, leaking low-level nuclear waste, and broken reactor vessel pumps.

• Every few minutes, furtively make a sound like a Geiger counter going off.

• When greeting the shift supervisor, be sure the other members of your tour group hear you remind him that you and he were once cell mates and ask him how long he's "been out on work release."

• Hum "Nearer My God to Thee" as you pass by the spent fuel rod containment section.

• Tell a group of first and second graders that the tour conductor will be happy to show them the room where mischievous children are treated to a scalding shower of superheated gamma rays, which will leave them with blistered cheeks and bursting eyeballs.

PBS Telethons

You can make a lasting first impression and an important charitable contribution at the same time by using these scandalously crude things to say and do at a PBS telethon.

- Promise to pledge a large amount of money only if the announcer sits up, begs, and grovels for your contribution.

If you're a pledge:

- Calmly advise the solicitor that "if this telethon doesn't end in the next two minutes I'm gonna blow up you, your transmission tower, Diana Rigg, Alistair Cooke, Dr. Who, and thousands of volunteers and pseudointellectual snobs."

- Scream, "Hey, I called you guys an hour ago! Where the hell's my pizza?"

- Offer to donate your sperm.

If you're soliciting contributions:

- Ask children in the audience to wait until their parents go to sleep and then take the green pieces of paper from their pocketbooks and wallets and mail them in.

- Bring in an old lady tied to a wheelchair, remind viewers of a certain 1940s movie with Victor Mature and Richard Widmark, and say, "I'm gonna take the old bat to a nearby rooming house and push her down the stairs unless you call in and pledge lots of dough."

- Offer an "incentive" bumper sticker that says WARNING: I DON'T BRAKE FOR NONPLEDGERS.

- Threaten to stay on the air forever unless contributions increase dramatically.

Parole Hearings

For a prison inmate, nothing is more important than the opportunity for early release. As a character witness, you can make the parole board's decision an easier one with these time-tested things to do and say at the next hearing.

• During the deliberation process, ask if the prisoner can play with his favorite plastic doll because "he may need it just in case he gets a little tense and has the urge to twist the head off something."

• Add weight to your letters recommending parole by adding the salutation "Yours in Satan."

• Advise the board that the prisoner's recent stabbing of a guard with a fork and steak knife was purely an accident and "could have happened to anyone who was running full speed in the general direction of the victim and accidentally tripped."

• Tell the board that if they agree to grant parole to Pam Smart, she promises "not to tell her students where you live."

- Notify board members that if they decide not to send him to a halfway house, Charles Manson would still like a "conjugal visit with Squeaky or one of your female relatives."

- Ask board members if they want their bribes delivered in unmarked tens and twenties in brown paper bags as usual.

- Dress up as a priest and tell the board that although you were originally troubled by the parolee's confession to several ax murders, "he's already said a couple of rosaries, and that seems punishment enough."

- Inform the board that, as the mother of the proposed parolee, you support a parole plan to have your son "go back to the old neighborhood, reconstruct his gang, pay off the loan shark, live in the basement of the poolroom, give illegal stimulants to horses at Aqueduct Racetrack, and do all he can to support his sixteen illegitimate kids."

- Hold up a sign that says DON'T BLAME ME—I VOTED FOR THE DEATH PENALTY.

Polka Parties

Polka parties offer a unique opportunity to antagonize both Polish-Americans and dance lovers. Put on your clean bowling shirt, grab an accordion, and practice these stridently tasteless things to do and say at your next soiree.

- Dress formally. For men that means suede shoes, pegged pants, ruffled tuxedo shirts, and satin dinner jackets that proclaim I'VE BEEN TO CRACOW. Women will need horsehair shawls, wooden platform shoes, new housecoats, and baggy support hose.

- Introduce yourself to strangers by saying, "I'm a professional pinsetter. What do you do?"

- Wear a button that exclaims I'M PROWD TO BEE POLLISH.

- Sell MY OTHER CAR'S A YUGO bumper stickers for $2.00 apiece or two for $6.00.

- Ask the bandleader to play the following hit polkas:

"I'll Polka You in the Mouth Polka"

"Someone Stole My Sleeveless T-Shirt Polka"

"Let's Kill Those Gypsies Polka"

"I Fell Off My Porch Again Polka"

"Don't Choke on the Kielbasa Polka"

"There Are No Bowl-o-Dromes in Heaven Polka"

"Don't Kiss Me, I'm Polish Polka"

"Snap the Chicken's Neck Quickly Polka"

"Who Stole the Bride's Bowling Shoes Polka"

"Get that Tuba Outta My Dupa Polka"

"Drop General Jarulzelski Down the Mine Shaft Polka"

Restaurants

Eat, drink, and be merry. And employ these infamously rank things to say and do the next time you eat out.

• Tell the manager you want to rent the banquet room for a get-together of the Molesters on Parole Support Group.

• When visiting the coat room, ask the attendant if you can also check your socks and Attends garments.

• If there's a long line ahead of you, find the spokesperson for the largest group and advise him that he'll have to rush home, "because there's been a death in your family."

• Practice the Heimlich maneuver on people who aren't choking.

• Ask for "the New York sirloin, please, but hold the hoof-and-mouth disease."

- Borrow the wine decanter from the adjacent table, explaining that you just don't have time to make it to the little boys' room.

- Tell the owner of a Chinese restaurant that you would like to interest him in a fast-food franchise called The Missing Kitty.

- Kid around with the waitress, inquiring, "How's the salmonella, I mean salmon, tonight?"

- Send a note to the owner indicating that you're a critic for the Mobil travel guides and that you've given his restaurant a "Sucks the Big One" rating.

- When tipping, use foreign money. An Argentinian fifty-dollar bill ought to be worth about thirty-five cents when exchanged for U.S. currency.

- Surreptitiously add "Road-Kill Kabob, $9.95" to the list of dinner specials.

Revival Meetings

Ever had a hankering to speak in tongues? You'll be fluent in no time after auditioning these disparagingly dreadful things to say and do at your next revival meeting.

• Suggest a Call Oral Home Contest and pledge not to send any more money to the ministry until he actually does bite the dust.

• Sell bumper stickers that say HONK IF YOU LIKE JESSICA'S NEW HONKERS.

• Visit Jim in prison. Tell him you've arranged for a conjugal visit with a born-again powerlifter.

• Send a group of prostitutes to picket Jimmy's pulpit while carrying signs saying WE'RE ALL IN IT FOR THE MONEY.

• Offer Pat a "baptism by fire" by dragging him on stage and then dropping him into a large caldron of boiling cooking oil.

- Follow Jesse around with a rubber duck and make it quack every time he starts to talk.

- Go on Oral's program and hand out leaflets that say CURE BACON, NOT PEOPLE and SAVE SHOES, NOT SOULS.

- When the collection plate is passed, steal as much money as possible. If you get caught, burst into tears and beg God and the viewing public for forgiveness.

- Wear a T-shirt that says JESUS IS COMING on the front and AND BOY IS HE PISSED on the back.

Road Trips

Just what you've been waiting for! An inspiring review of intolerably debauched things to say and do when you travel by car.

- Display a bumper sticker that says MY OTHER CAR IS A HEARSE.

- When a police officer pulls you over remember the following:

    1. If you're asked to take a breath test, burp.

    2. Answer the request for your license and registration by saying, "I'm not sure where they are; I think the car is stolen."

    3. When the officer asks you to get out of the car and perform some field sobriety tests, respond, "Since Mars is entering the moons of Jupiter in my astroplane, I won't be able to honor your request until late next week. I hope that won't inconvenience you."

90

- To avoid monotony while driving at night, alternately use no lights, bright lights, and fog lights every twenty to thirty seconds.

- In bumper-to-bumper traffic, drive on median strips, breakdown lanes, sidewalks, and lawns.

- Converse with carpoolers and hitchhikers by providing animated descriptions of the Hillside Strangler case, Charles Manson's cult, and the latest unsolved torture murder.

- Discourage tailgating by displaying a bumper sticker that says DON'T LAUGH, I'M RELOADING.

- Find out how close, in millimeters, you can get the front bumper of your car to the rear fender of a motorcycle before the driver decides to eject.

- Reassign the point value in the Pedestrians Run-over Game by adding ten points for nuns and Scientologists and subtracting five points for bag ladies and water-meter readers.

- Indicate your intention to take a left turn by suddenly braking, putting on the right-turn indicator, and backing across a median strip and two lanes of traffic.

- Keep other motorists in their own lane by painting HOMICIDAL PAROLEE on the lid of your trunk.

- If you accidentally rear end somebody, hop out of your car and insist that the car in front backed into you.

• After any accident, move the injured only if you need to relieve them of their wallets or expensive jewelry, or you want to shut up their annoying complaints of pain.

Rock Concerts

Music, sex, drugs, and mayhem. The only way to further enhance the rock-concert experience is to follow these screamingly coarse suggestions.

- If security personnel try to frisk you, say, "Not here, not now, we've hardly met."

- When women throw their underwear on stage, tell the band to cover the microphones with it in order to drown out their music.

- Get total backstage access by wearing an ID tag that says I SELL DRUGS TO THE BAND.

- Wear a dayglow orange TIPPER GORE IN '92 button.

- Pass a note to Michael Jackson telling him you're willing to sell him Elvis Presley's corpse "for the right price."

- Ask Paul Simon whether Art Garfunkel's hairstyle had anything to do with the break-up.

- Ask, "What group of sluglike cretins has been hired as security for this concert?"

Small-Claims Court

When you really want to exact that pound of flesh, it's best to go to court and get it for yourself. Whether you're the plaintiff or the defendant, you'll be sure to make an impression at your next municipal court hearing with these obnoxiously horrid things to say and do.

- Ask the clerk to call your case when the other party is in the men's room.

- Pretend you don't know any better and say, "Hey, who's the loser in the black nightgown?"

- Even if he's wearing a name tag, keep calling the bailiff "Rusty" and tell him he reminds you of Barney Fife on the old Andy Griffith show.

- When the oath is being administered and the clerk asks, "Do you swear?," say "Yes, frequently, and often it involves my bizarre and sadistic sexual proclivities."

- Bring in a parrot trained to say, "Objection over-ruled!" when the other party objects, and "Objection sustained!" whenever you object.

- If you're the defendant, whenever your name's mentioned, jump up and say, "No, not me, I was in Buffalo that night! I've got three witnesses to say I was in Buffalo that night. There's no way they're gonna hang that one on me."

- During a recess, approach the other party's star witness with this information:

  1. His car's on fire in the parking lot.

  2. Ed McMahon called with a big surprise and he ought to go home immediately.

  3. Your four-hundred-pound Cousin Rocco suggests that if the witness doesn't have a memory failure soon, he'll "have to learn to walk all over again."

Sonny Bono Campaign Rallies

Help a sixties beatnik ease into the political arena with these grotesquely indelicate things to say and do out on the Sonny Bono campaign trail.

• Take Sonny aside and gently explain that he's "the only Democratic candidate who could make Dan Quayle look good."

• Keep telling Sonny that PAC men are political fundraisers, not video game cannibals.

• Urge Sonny not to wear his high-heeled boots, bell-bottom jeans, mood rings, and flowered shirts on "Meet the Press."

• Beg Sonny to invite Cher to the national DAR Convention so she can sing such crowd-pleasing hits as "Bang Bang," "Gypsies, Tramps and Thieves," and "Half-Breed."

• Explain to Sonny that the term *running mate* does not refer to his jogging partner.

Stress Management Seminars

Can't take the pressure anymore? That's OK because you can now use these time-tested methods for letting it all out at your next stress management seminar.

• During group sessions, don't be shy about discussing your background, making sure to emphasize your murder of your parents, your involuntary commitment to a hospital for the criminally insane, and the marginal success of the drug therapy and electric shock treatments you've undergone.

• Share techniques with your group that have proved particularly successful in helping you to relax:

    1. making death threats in calligraphy;

    2. repeatedly punching animate objects;

    3. tampering with over-the-counter medications;

    4. staging toy train wrecks; and

5. designing a custom-made electric chair for your ex-spouse.

• Practice visual relaxation by focusing on the restful image of the New Kids on the Block being strangled with baling wire.

• Recommend that participants relieve their stress by listening to an audiotape of these soothing sounds:

> **1.** two Domino's Pizza trucks crossing a double yellow line at 60 miles per hour and hitting each other in a head-on crash;
>
> **2.** the long, deep, hollow grinding noise of an older-model dental drill;
>
> **3.** the Berlin Symphony playing the Brahms "Lullaby" by sliding their fingernails down differently pitched blackboards to obtain just the right note and pitch; or
>
> **4.** a laser-guided Hellfire missile exploding inside an Iraqi tank turret.

Tanning Salons

Here are some incineratingly caustic suggestions for making a memorable impression the next time you go to tan your hide.

• Suggest that the salon owner consider changing the name of the establishment from Tans R Us to Brains R Damaged.

• Quiz an attendant about the difference between "bake" and "broil" temperature settings.

• Advise the salon manager that if she gets any darker, she'll soon be mistaken for a Hottentot.

• Inform the attendant that you don't need a timer because you'll know that you're well-done when your toenails begin to bubble.

• Reassure fellow customers that "if the eye protection doesn't work there's a white cane, dark glasses, and braille book in the back room."

Tattoo Parlors

Tattoo parlors are sure to replace gyms and singles bars as the "in" spots of the 1990s. You'll meet lots of fascinating people there, including drunken sailors, drug-crazed bikers, state health inspectors, middle-aged ad executives, bad actors, and fortyish strippers. Revel in these indecently unseemly things to say or do the next time you venture into a tattoo parlor.

- Ask the tattoo artist if both of his parents were cretins.

- Insist that the tattoo artist spell *mother* with an *o* rather than a *u*.

- Point out that Edsels were probably still popular the last time the needle was cleaned.

- Sidle up to a biker, elbow him hard in the kidney, and announce, "DEA—are you holding?"

- Engage the tattoo artist in friendly chatter by saying, "Let me guess something about you: you've got a prison record, you love your Harley, your girlfriend has had group sex with most of your male friends, your wallet is chained to your back pocket even though it contains only twenty-eight bucks, and you've taken at least one shower in the past five years."

• Tell the artist that you want Leonardo da Vinci's *Last Supper* tattooed on your chest, and you want it in color, with Judas asking the waitress for separate checks.

Texas Chainsaw Massacres

Leatherface, Granpa, and other relatives are desperate for company. You'll make a big impression on them by making these cutting comments when you attend their next chainsaw massacre.

- Ask Granpa who does his dental work.

- Practice these three sure-fire conversation starters when you meet up with Leatherface:

    1. "Leatherface, is that your first or last name?"

    2. "May I suggest that your relationship with your mother may be at the root of all this?"

    3. "Wouldn't a plastic Nixon mask be just as effective?"

- Tell the family you'll "do lunch" only if they improve their table manners.

- Ask Granpa if he'd consider wearing a FRIENDS FOREVER heart-shaped leather apron.

- Promise Granpa you won't tell him how to do a massacre if he promises not to tell you how to set a table.

- Advise family members that you're from the noise abatement department and they're going to "have to turn down that chainsaw."

- Caution Leatherface that he still seems to have a problem pronouncing his vowels and that when he gets excited he should put down his chainsaw, take a deep breath, and enunciate fully before beginning a murderous rampage.

- Inform Granpa that his chances for a Friday night date look dim because there aren't many "hook and pull" nights at singles bars.

Train Derailments

There are now three things in life you can absolutely count on: death, taxes, and train derailments. Call your insurance agent first and then try out these unbelievably abominable things to say and do during your next train trip.

• When boarding the train, ask the conductor how many times the engineer has failed the random drug test.

• Circulate a petition to change the regular train whistle to a pipe-organ rendition of Chopin's "funeral march."

• Ask the service personnel, "How many decades ago did someone check the brakes on this death trap?"

• When surrendering your ticket to the conductor, ask where you turn in your coupon for a free body bag.

• Regale club car patrons with tales of fiery train wrecks caused by stale croissants left on the tracks.

• Encourage fellow travelers to throw themselves across the seats and cry plaintively—"just for practice."

• Lead fellow passengers in a rousing rendition of "The Old Wreck of the 98."

• Go to the club car and ask for a dozen can openers, noting that "they'll come in handy when this thing gets telescoped into a crumpled mass of twisted metal and grinding steel."

• When the bar car is finally closed for the evening, insist on visiting the engineer because "he'll have something to help me calm my nerves."

• Tell the conductor that you're writing a book about the subject and you want to know why a disproportionately large number of sociopaths, drug addicts, and mentally ill people managed to be hired as engineers.

• Suggest that the company create a "frequent survivor" mileage plan.

Triathlons

Triathlons offer a great chance to show poor sportsmanship and rudeness of an extremely high order. Since winning is the most important thing, don't hesitate to enhance your prospects by taking full advantage of these suggestions at your next triathlon.

- Host an all-you-can-eat beans and beer blowout the night before the race.

- While warming up for the three-kilometer swim, spray shark attractant on competitors' swim goggles.

- Stick leeches on the neck of the bicyclist in front of you.

- Have your friends plant false finish lines and phony detours throughout the racecourse.

- Replace competitors' sneaker laces with strands of linguine.

- Carry a walking stick and trip runners when no one else is looking.

- Throw a fake diamondback at fellow runners and yell, "Snake!!"

- Tell the runner in front of you that he's got "a helluva rash" on the back of his leg.

- When bystanders and supporters hand you a cup of water, throw it back in their faces, saying, "Where's my Evian?"

- Right before a steep ascent, assure competitors that "it's all downhill from here."

- Badger other runners with questions such as "Aren't you beginning to cramp yet?" or "Hey, look at the size of that guy's charley horse!"

- Secretly fill the standby oxygen tanks with carbon monoxide.

TV Game Show and Talk Show Tapings

Rudeness is a certain cure for the endless vapid patter of game show and talk show hosts. Therefore these awesomely loutish things to say and do at your next taping are recommended.

- Audition for "Wheel of Fortune" by putting a propeller on your zipper with a sign that says WHEE! SPIN THIS!

- Admire Alex Trebek's wardrobe and point out that you weren't aware that Frederick's of Hollywood made trousers.

- Advise Bryant Gumbel that "Deborah will spill her guts on 'A Current Affair' " unless he forks over a million dollars in unmarked new bills.

- Remind Chuck Woolery who he is.

Unemployment Lines

Unemployment lines are unfortunately a sad but natural by-product of a weak economy. Make the most of the opportunity by demonstrating your deplorably low-rent manners at the unemployment office.

- Any time an unemployment counselor says something you don't like, hit her with a rubber truncheon.

- Tell the benefits coordinator that your brother's a crop duster and if you don't get your first unemployment check within twenty minutes, her house will receive a lethal dose of chlordane.

- Clear out the line in front of you by employing any of these foolproof tactics:

    1. planting a bogus story about cops sticking "numerous tickets on that red Chevette out front";

    2. circulating the rumor that they're hiring at the Beef 'n Barf;

3. announcing that the blood bank down the street is paying twenty-five bucks a quart;

4. displaying a laminated photo ID card that says, I'M A SCHIZO RAPIST AND BY ORDER OF THE CRIMINAL DIVISION OF THE SUPERIOR COURT I MUST WEAR THIS IDENTIFICATION TAG AT ALL TIMES; or

5. sticking the guy in front of you with a hat pin and saying, "Thanks for holding my place in line."

• Tell the interviewer that your brother's a city councilman and if the interviewer doesn't "smarten up" he'll be cleaning filters at the sewage treatment plant very soon.

• Bring along a high-strung Doberman for companionship and advise staff members that you need to get a job because "Spike's hungry."

• If you're denied benefits, walk to the supervisor's desk with a cage containing six gerbils. Tell him that you left your house with ten gerbils and that you'll eat one every half hour until you get a check.

Vacation Villa Shakedowns

Those pesky vacation-home salespeople are at it again. They want to sell you a second home in some malaria-infested swamp down South or an unirrigated desert out West. Use these demonically loathsome comebacks to resist the next vacation-villa sales pitch.

- Ask if your home will be built on solid marshland or old Belgian newspapers.

- Identify yourself as an investigator from the Securities and Exchange Commission, explain the penalties involving fraud, and then introduce your friend as "the FBI agent who'll be arresting you now."

- Demand to know how long they've been building "these glorified lean-tos."

- Seek out important information about the development by asking:

    1. "How many insects are there per square inch?"

    2. "When do you plan to put out the swamp

fire that's already destroyed several dozen townhouse condos?"

3. "Why are all the exterior walls and siding made from recycled plastic spoons?"

• Inform the salesperson that you appreciate the wide range of color choices, but it's tough to decide between the tawny beige, light brown beige, tan beige, and cocoa beige.

• Ask the social director if the development has its own coven.

• Tell the salesperson that you've studied the plans closely and are curious as to how they can get sixty-seven five-room ranch homes on a single three-acre tract.

• Admire the "individuality" of each of the development's homes, noting that there are at least three variations of doorknobs and that the slope of the driveway of two of the houses is at a degree or two greater than the others.

• Remark that "there's probably no need for a formal garbage disposal system with so many crocodiles in the neighborhood."

• Suggest that a financing provision of 35 percent APR monthly is a little bit higher than what you had planned to spend.

• When signing the application form, point out that you're a practicing cannibal and that federal law forbids discrimination against you.

Wakes and Funerals

A truly boorish mind can pay dividends when it comes to wakes and funerals. Bid a fond farewell to discretion and restraint as you follow these death-defying suggestions when rubbing elbows with the dark angel.

- Adults can be notified by phone or in person of a recent death like so:

> **1.** "Martha, have you heard the expression 'he bought the farm'?"

> **2.** "Susan, do you remember what happened to Patrick Swayze in *Ghost*?"

Breaking the bad news to children, however, requires a special touch. For example:

> **1.** "No sense in waiting up for Uncle Vito, Bobby. He's sleeping with the fishes tonight."

> **2.** "Billy, come over and sit on my lap. Remember when I told you the story about Mr. Grim Reaper? Well, last night he came to our house about the same time Dad grabbed the

butane lighter, went to look for the gas leak, and . . ."

- Hire a florist to deliver a wreath of carnations bearing the message, "From his favorite mistress."

- Offer to prepare the obituary and then punch it up with funny stories about marital infidelity, money missing from an employer's trust account, and an upcoming exposé on "A Current Affair."

- Choose an appropriately touching sympathy card with an appropriately up-to-date rhyme such as

> Roses are red,
> Dahlias are black,
> Sorry your son Ralph
> Got stabbed in the back.

- Recommend that the widow be "ecologically aware" by doing away with the casket entirely and either burying the deceased in a jumbo biodegradable plastic bag or just wrapping him up in a lot of newspapers.

- Resist the bereaved family's plans for a backyard burial by reminding them of what happened in *Poltergeist*.

- Send out invitations to all mourners telling them you're having a "costume wake," and they should come dressed up as their favorite dead person.

- Prepare an obituary stating that in lieu of flowers, contributions should be made to the Save the Satanist Children's Fund or a neo-Nazi youth group.

- Tell the undertaker that because the deceased had "a special sense of humor," you want him to dress up as Giggles the Clown.

- Advise the widow that the death certificate appears to be forged.

- While attending the wake, make sure to ask the funeral director one of these questions in a thundering voice:

    1. "Where's my cut?"

    2. "You really think you'll be able to beat that necrophilia rap?"

- Sign the guest register "Jimmy Hoffa" or "Amelia Earhart."

- Replace Old Age clichés with New Age frankness, like so:

    1. "She looks just like she's dead."

    2. "Be thankful he went quickly before he put a big hole in your bank account."

- At an open-casket wake, ask if you can have a foot pedal on the floor to flip the casket lid open or closed, depending on the individual preference of the mourner, and just to circulate the air in case it gets a little stuffy in the funeral parlor.

- If the deceased died owing you money, rifle his pockets while he's in the casket.

116

- When it's a closed-casket wake, loudly argue with the undertaker, saying, "I just want to make sure it's really him and this isn't some phony insurance scam."

- At an open-casket wake, approach the deceased, pull up a chair, sit down, and ask questions such as:

    1. "How are you?"

    2. "Where are you going on vacation?"

    3. "Catch that Mets game last night?"

    4. "Cold enough for you?"

- Give the widower a small gift as a token of respect, such as a cookbook entitled *Cooking for One*.

- Tie a boot and a bucket to the rear bumper of the hearse.

- Request that the organist play the following songs at the church service:

    "One Less Bell to Answer"

    "Roll over Beethoven"

    "Breathless"

- Remind the undertaker that the deceased was a "car nut" so that when he wheels the casket into the church, he should "lay on a lot of rubber and do a wheelie or two."

- When you're a pallbearer and the casket is halfway down the church steps, start yelling, "Wait a minute, I think I hear somebody coughing in there!"